Forest Fires

Sandra Woodcock

Published in association with The Basic Skills Agency

Hodder & Stoughton

A MEMBER OF THE HODDER HEADLINE GROUP

Acknowledgements

Cover: Raymond Gehman/Corbis

Photos: p 4 © Craig Aurness/Corbis; pp 8, 15, 18 © The Press Association Ltd 1999; p 11 © Anthony Bannister, Gallo Images/Corbis; p23 © Reuters News Media Inc./Corbis; p 26 © Mark Gibson/Corbis; p 28 © Layne Kennedy/Corbis.

Every effort has been made to trace copyright holders of material reproduced in this book. Any rights not acknowledged will be acknowledged in subsequent printings if notice is given to the publisher.

Orders: please contact Bookpoint Ltd, 39 Milton Park, Abingdon, Oxon OX14 4TD. Telephone (44) 01235 400414, Fax: (44) 01235 400454. Lines are open from 9.00–6.00, Monday to Saturday, with a 24 hour message answering service. Email address: orders@bookpoint.co.uk

British Library Cataloguing in Publication Data
A catalogue record for this title is available from the British Library

ISBN 0 340 80065 8

First published 2001
Impression number   10 9 8 7 6 5 4 3 2 1
Year   2007 2006 2005 2004 2003 2002 2001

Copyright © 2001 Sandra Woodcock

Typeset by SX Composing DTP, Rayleigh, Essex.
Printed in Great Britain for Hodder & Stoughton Educational, a division of Hodder Headline Plc, 338 Euston Road, London NW1 3BH by Redwood Books Ltd, Trowbridge, Wilts.

Contents

		Page
1	Fear of Fire	1
2	Forest Fires	6
3	How do Forest Fires Start?	10
4	Firebombers	14
5	Fire Fighters	17
6	Fire on Storm King Mountain	22
7	Fire as a Tool	25

1 Fear of Fire

It was a hot day in August 1961.
In a forest in North America
a group of men were in great danger.
They were fire fighters.
They had parachuted into the forest
where a fire had been started by lightning.
Strong winds hit the area.
The fire 'exploded like a blow torch'

Twenty men made their way
to a burned area of the forest.
They had cans of water
they had been using to fight the fire.
Now they tore up their T-shirts
and soaked them in water
to put around their heads.
They did not panic
but they feared for their lives.

Above their heads,
a huge cloud had formed
from the heat and winds of the fire.
Lightning was coming down near them.
Flames roared all around them.
The wind was gusting at 40–50 mph
Then, in the smoke above their heads,
they saw something.

They thought it was a tree falling on them.
But they were looking at the skids of a helicopter.
They had not heard the engine
because of the noise of the fire.
The helicopter dropped down
as the fire moved closer.

Being a firefighter is a very dangerous job.

He flew out two men at a time.
But the area was getting hotter.
It was hard to control the helicopter.
So the pilot took four men at a time:
two inside and two holding on to the skids!
In this way, all 20 men were plucked from the fire.

The fire was at Higgins Ridge.
The pilot was Rod Snider.
He was given a medal for bravery.
The men were smokejumpers:
expert fire fighters who drop into
the most difficult fires.
Within a few days, most of them
were jumping again.
There were new fires to fight.

2 Forest Fires

Fire out of control in a hot dry forest
is very frightening.
But every year in some parts of the world
dangerous fires burn out of control.
In 1997, forest fires burning in Indonesia
caused many problems.
In 1998, more than a thousand fires burned
in Mexico and Central America.
In Greece and Italy
there are fires almost every summer.

Fire can destroy huge areas of land and timber.
Smoke from forest fires
can cause health problems and pollution.
If the fires come close to towns,
there is a danger to peoples' lives
and to their homes.
In the USA, Canada and Australia
much money is spent on managing fire.

A dangerous fire burning out of control destroying land and timber.

Forest fires can affect the whole of the planet.
Very hot fires burn at 1000°C or more.
They burn up carbon from the forest floor
and even burn down into the soil.
The smoke contains gases
which are making our planet hotter.

Satellites in space
monitor the Earth's weather.
Images from the satellites
show forest fires burning across the globe.
Fires even burn in areas where there are no people.

3 How do Forest Fires Start?

Forest fires burn in hot dry weather.
They burn faster if there is a wind.
A long dry spell
means that grass and plants are dry.
This makes good fuel.
Some trees have oils that make the fires hotter.

Many fires are caused
by people being careless.
A campfire that wasn't put out
or a glowing cigarette end
can set fire to dry areas.
Some fires are started
by lightning strikes.

This man is starting a fire on purpose to get rid of grass and to create a fire break.

Some fires are started on purpose.
In some countries
people want more land for building.
The law may not allow them
to clear forests.
If a forest fire breaks out,
the land is cleared.
It can then be used for other things.
Some people think that this was the reason
for the fires in Greece.
In Indonesia, fires were started in land disputes
between farmers and foresters.

Forest fires may start and spread on the ground.
They become more dangerous
when the flames spread across the tops of the trees.
As the fire gets hotter
it can become a firestorm.
A firestorm cannot be stopped.
It has to burn itself out
by destroying everything in the area
that can burn.

4 Firebombers

Planes have been used in fire fighting
since the 1940s.
At first they used special bags full of water.
They dropped the 'water bombs'
through holes in the cabin.
By the 1950s the planes
could scoop up water from lakes
and dump it in front of the fire.

A plane used in fire fighting, dropping a 'water bomb' on the fire below.

Today there are super 'waterbombers'
The Helitanker can carry
2,000 gallons (7,500 litres) of water
in one trip.
It can refill in 45 seconds.

The biggest waterbomber has tanks
with 11,000 gallons (42,000 litres).
It can be filled and ready for take off
in 15 minutes.
It can reach a fire anywhere in the world
within 12 hours.

5 Fire Fighters

Fighting fire needs bravery and skill.
There are teams of men and women
who are trained to fight forest and wildland fires.
They need to be ready to go
to any area where a fire is out of control.
Some will clear land to make a fireline.
They use chain saws and shovels
to clear away anything
that can feed the fire.
They clear a line
all around the burning area.

Fighting fire needs bravery and skill.

Sometimes fire is used to fight fire.
The teams may decide
to light a controlled fire.
They burn plants and bushes
ahead of the wildfire.
This is risky and needs special care.

In the USA the most skilled of these teams
are called Hotshots.
They can work in remote areas
for a long time.
They are often called in
when fire first starts.

Sometimes fire fighters
cannot get close to the problem.
Special fire fighters called smokejumpers
may be called in.
Smokejumpers parachute
into a fire area from planes.
They have some tools with them
and the planes drop more gear to help them.
In forest fires, the smokejumpers drop
into narrow gaps between the trees.

Another way of getting down to the fire
is to shin down ropes from the planes.
The people who do this are called rappellers.
A good rappeller
can drop 250 feet down a half-inch rope
in about 15 seconds.
Smoke jumping and rappelling
is dangerous work.
The aim is to get in
before a fire gets too big.
But fire can flare out of control in minutes.
The smokejumpers can get trapped
in flames that may be 80 feet high.

6   Fire on Storm King Mountain

Fire fighters have to be strong and very fit.
They may be fighting fire
for many days and nights, with little rest.
The fire fighters are hired just for the season.
They work in the months
when most wildfires happen.
They may have other jobs.
Many are students.
But they come back year after year.
They build up their skills and experience.

Sometimes there is a tragedy.
One of the worst in the USA was in 1994
on Storm King Mountain, Colorado.
The area had been hit
by 5,600 lightening strikes.
Fires started.
The one on Storm King Mountain was the worst.
The fire burned for four days.
Then on 6 July, a team of smokejumpers
and Hotshots went in.

Forest fires can burn for days, destroying everything
in their path.

But the fire suddenly changed.
It became a blow up.
This is the fire fighter's nightmare.
The fire moves from the surface
to the tree tops.

The fire became more intense, moved faster
and the flames got higher.
Fourteen fire fighters
were trapped and died in the fire.
They were experts, but they became victims
of the terrible power of fire.

7   Fire as a Tool

Fire can destroy so much.
It's hard to think of it as useful.
But forest managers don't spend
all their time and money fighting fire.
They know that some fire can be helpful.

On the forest floor
there can be a build up
of dead leaves and grass.
There can be too many
young plants and trees.
This is dangerous
If a fire started, it would burn quickly.
So it is good to let some fires
burn under control.
Small fires can be used
to clear the forest waste.
This helps to stop bigger fires from spreading.

A fire burning under control to clear the forest waste of
dead leaves and grass.

Fire is part of the natural life of the forest.
Some trees, like the jack pine,
can only grow when their seeds have been burned.
After a fire, the soil is better.
New grass and plants grow quickly.
More animals come into the area.

To people who look after forests
the problem of fire is not simple.
Fire is sometimes good and sometimes bad.
Fighting fire is only part of the answer.

New plants and grass growing quickly in a forest after a
fire.